The Wayland Library of Science and Technology

THE ENVIRONMENT

CLINT TWIST

Wayland

The Wayland Library of Science and Technology

The Nature of Matter
The Universal Forces
Stars and Galaxies
The Solar System
The Changing Landscape
Air and Oceans
Origins of Life
The Science of Life
Plants and Animals
Animal Behaviour
The Human Machine
Health and Medicine

The Environment
Feeding the World
Raw Materials
Manufacturing Industry
Energy Sources
The Power Generators
Transport
Space Travel
Communications
The Computer Age
Scientific Instruments
Towards Tomorrow

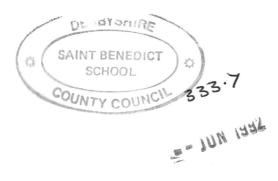

Advisory Series Editor
Robin Kerrod

Consultant
Professor R. Terry

Editor: Caroline Sheldrick
Design: Cooper-Wilson
Picture Research: Alison Renney
Production: Steve Elliott
Art Director: John Ridgeway
Project Director: Lawrence Clarke

First published in 1990 by
Wayland (Publishers) Ltd
61 Western Road, Hove
East Sussex BN3 1JD, England

AN EQUINOX BOOK

Planned and produced by:
Equinox (Oxford) Limited
Musterlin House, Jordan Hill Road,
Oxford OX2 8DP

British Library Cataloguing in Publication Data
Twist, Clint
    The environment.
    1. Environment
    I. Title
    333.7

ISBN 0-7502-0020-0

Media conversion and typesetting by Peter
MacDonald, Vanessa Hersey and Una Macnamara
Origination by Hong Kong Reprohouse Co Ltd
Printed in Italy by Rotolito Lombarda
S.p.A., Milan
Bound in France by AGM

Front cover: The cityscape of Manhattan, New
York, USA by night.
Back cover: A racoon raiding a dustbin.

Contents

Introduction

Human beings live on a very crowded planet; we share the Earth with about 30 million other species. The study of life in its natural environment is called ecology. Ecologists study the relationships between species, and their behaviour.

Human feeding, directly or indirectly, has been responsible for centuries of accumulated damage to the environment. Whole landscapes have been transformed by the axe and the plough, and much wildlife has been hunted out of existence.

For over 300 years, we have been recording extinctions: the disappearance of entire species. Thousands of species are now endangered.

Human beings also bear responsibility for polluting the environment with chemicals. Some are deadly poisons, some may alter the climate of the whole planet; all of them in some way threaten the future of the Earth.

◄ The skyline of Manhattan, New York, USA, by night. One of the most crowded places on Earth, the city shows how successful humans have been in colonizing the planet. But how costly is our success?

Nature in balance

▶ City schoolchildren pond-dipping in Essex, England. Environmental education is becoming more common in many countries. Concern is growing about the many threats to wildlife and the balance of nature posed by the growth of industry and human populations. Young people are especially keen to play their part in restoring the natural balance.

No living organism exists in complete isolation from others. Plants and animals that live in a particular place share the same air, the same rocks and the same neighbours. They live together, and they live in harmony. Some feed on others, but the larger picture is one of overall balance.

Scientific studies have shown that this balance is achieved through an extremely complex network of relationships between different species. One of the most important relationships is that between plants and animals. Without plants, animal life would be impossible.

Ecology

Levels of study in ecology

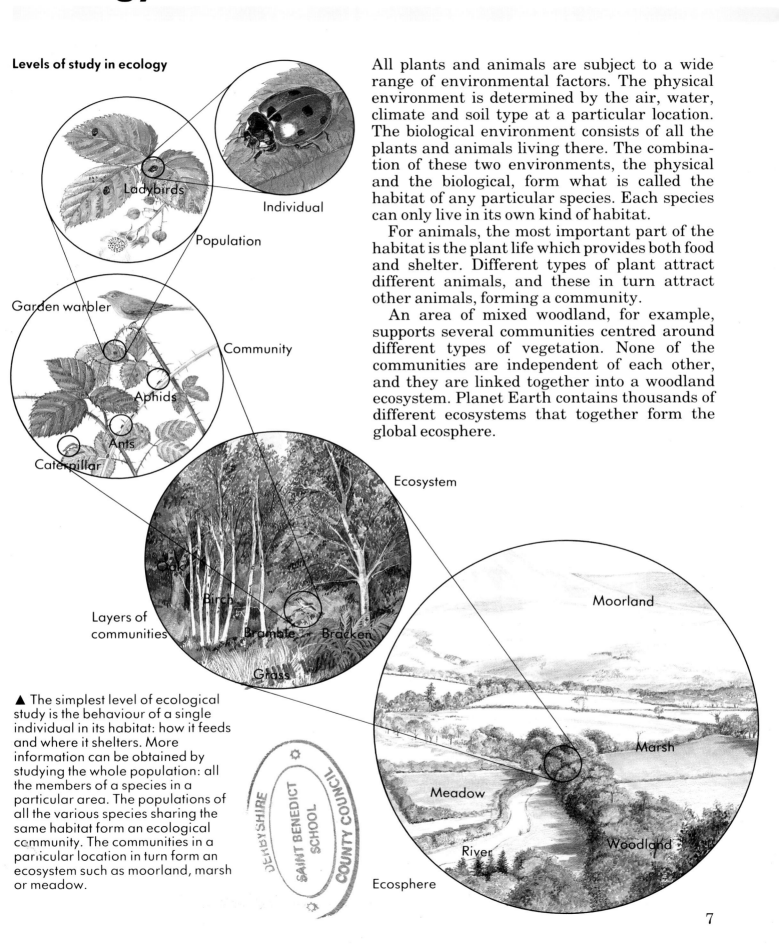

Individual

Population

Ladybirds

Garden warbler

Community

Aphids

Ants

Caterpillar

Ecosystem

Layers of communities

Oak

Birch

Bramble · Bracken

Grass

Moorland

Marsh

Meadow

River

Woodland

Ecosphere

All plants and animals are subject to a wide range of environmental factors. The physical environment is determined by the air, water, climate and soil type at a particular location. The biological environment consists of all the plants and animals living there. The combination of these two environments, the physical and the biological, form what is called the habitat of any particular species. Each species can only live in its own kind of habitat.

For animals, the most important part of the habitat is the plant life which provides both food and shelter. Different types of plant attract different animals, and these in turn attract other animals, forming a community.

An area of mixed woodland, for example, supports several communities centred around different types of vegetation. None of the communities are independent of each other, and they are linked together into a woodland ecosystem. Planet Earth contains thousands of different ecosystems that together form the global ecosphere.

▲ The simplest level of ecological study is the behaviour of a single individual in its habitat: how it feeds and where it shelters. More information can be obtained by studying the whole population: all the members of a species in a particular area. The populations of all the various species sharing the same habitat form an ecological community. The communities in a particular location in turn form an ecosystem such as moorland, marsh or meadow.

Themes in ecology

Ecology is the study of how species react to other species. By studying the relationships and interactions between species in a community, ecologists can learn how a balance is maintained in nature. The feeding behaviour of animals is one of the most important interactions. Plants can meet their own needs from sunlight, carbon dioxide, water and nutrients in the soil. Animals, however, have actively to search for food, since they cannot make their own.

An area of woodland may support a population of millions of flying insects. These offer a rich source of food for airborne predators able to catch them on the wing. This role is filled by certain birds and bats. A position within an ecosystem such as this is called a niche.

Animals may feed on the caterpillars of the same insects, but occupy a different niche. Similarly, the birds and bats occupy different niches because the birds hunt by day and the bats by night. This separation of niches avoids unnecessary competition for food. In general, each potential niche tends to be occupied by only one or two different species. Any more would make an imbalance.

Feeding behaviour is central to defining a niche, but other interactions are also very important to the ecosystem. Many animals are essential to plant reproduction. Insects fertilize flowers while feeding, and birds and mammals are used by plants to carry seeds great distances. Some interactions are extremely specific, and occur only between two species; others involve many species.

▲ The African Bushveld elephant shrew specializes in eating termites, an abundant source of food. The behaviour of any species is largely determined by its habitat.

◄ The giraffe occupies a very successful niche on the African plains. Its long neck enables it to feed on vegetation that is above other animals' heads.

Flamingo   Sheld

Succession

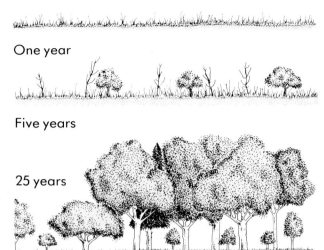

One year

Five years

25 years

When new land is created, or old land is cleared, a new community is born. The first living colonists will be plants suited to the open conditions. Plants are vital in forming and shaping a habitat. Their roots hold the soil together, and a mass of vegetation can moderate the effects of harsh climates. As the first community develops, it creates the shelter and shade necessary to nurture the next group of less hardy plants.

This progressive occupation of land is known as succession. Different types of vegetation follow distinctive patterns of succession. It may take hundreds of years for plants to turn these sand dunes into firm ground. After one year, grasses have already taken root. After five years, shrubs and small trees are established. After 25 years, the process is well under way, though far from complete.

Ecosystems do not suddenly come into existence; they are the result of many centuries of evolution. A community, on the other hand, can form during a much shorter period of time. Usually, the community will go through a series of stages before reaching its final form, which is known as a climax community. Whatever the ecosystem – prairie, tundra, woodland or jungle – a climax community will regenerate itself indefinitely under natural conditions. If a small part is damaged, it soon builds up again.

The first inhabitants of a community, which are known as pioneer species, arrive as wind-borne seeds and flying insects. On coasts and islands they may also be washed up by the sea.

At first there are relatively few interactions. As the community develops, other species may displace the pioneers, only to be displaced themselves as succession continues. Climax communities usually contain a wide variety of plant or animal species, linked by a very complex network of interactions.

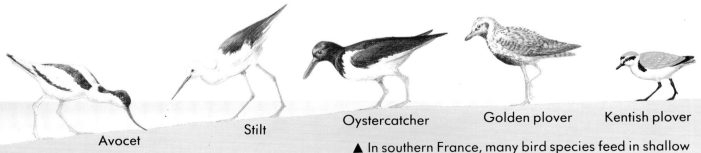

Avocet

Stilt

Oystercatcher

Golden plover

Kentish plover

▲ In southern France, many bird species feed in shallow lagoons. The length of beak, neck and legs determine the depth of water each can reach, and therefore the feeding niche of each species.

Food webs

The source of all food and living energy is the Sun. By studying feeding habits, ecologists can trace the flow of energy through an ecosystem. The process of photosynthesis enables plants to manufacture their own food. For this reason, plants are called primary producers.

Animals that feed directly on plants (herbivores) are known as primary consumers. Animals that obtain their food from other animals (carnivores) are called secondary consumers. These different levels of feeding can be linked together into a food chain which always begins with a form of vegetation. The stages in the chain are often described as belonging to different trophic levels.

Food chains link together individual plant and animal species. The various food chains within an ecosystem can be combined to create a much more complex food web. At the summit of the food web are the top predators, whose food energy may have passed through as many as five different organisms. The final connections in the food web are the decomposers. These are the bacteria and fungi that break down dead organic matter into its component parts and return the nutrients to the environment.

Food web in a temperate lake

- First trophic level (primary producers)
- Second trophic level (herbivores)
- Third trophic level
- Fourth trophic level
- Fifth trophic level
- Sixth trophic level

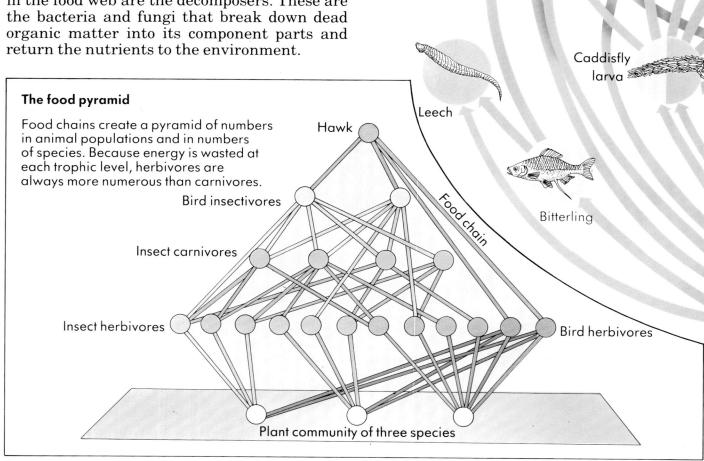

Duck

Frog/tadpole

Leech

Caddisfly larva

Bitterling

Food chain

The food pyramid

Food chains create a pyramid of numbers in animal populations and in numbers of species. Because energy is wasted at each trophic level, herbivores are always more numerous than carnivores.

Hawk

Bird insectivores

Insect carnivores

Insect herbivores

Bird herbivores

Plant community of three species

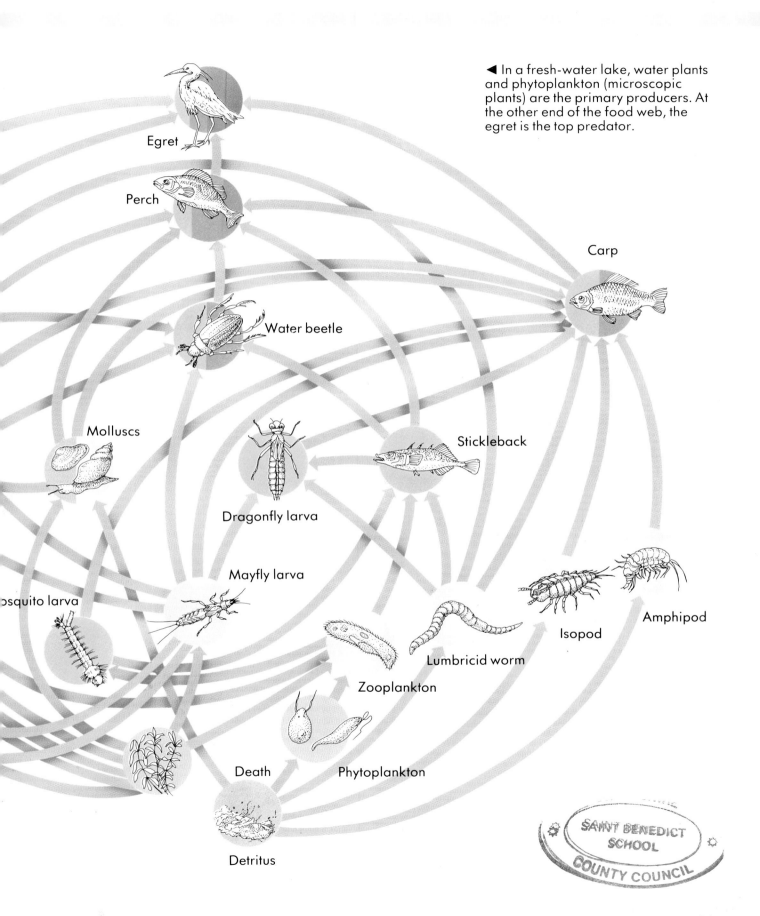

Egret

Perch

Carp

Water beetle

Molluscs

Dragonfly larva

Stickleback

Mayfly larva

Mosquito larva

Amphipod

Isopod

Lumbricid worm

Zooplankton

Phytoplankton

Death

Detritus

◄ In a fresh-water lake, water plants and phytoplankton (microscopic plants) are the primary producers. At the other end of the food web, the egret is the top predator.

In the rain forest

The rain forests of South America, Africa and South-east Asia are among the most complex ecosystems that exist. The hot, wet conditions have encouraged the development of an incredible variety of species. More than half the species on Earth may be found in these forests. This diversity of life is one of the main characteristics of these ecosystems.

The unvarying climate ensures a year-round supply of fruit and flowers. The variety of habitats and food sources provide countless opportunities for primary consumers. These in turn create niches for carnivores. In general, populations tend to be small, with many species existing in self-contained "island" communities.

A layered environment
The rain forests form a multi-layered, three-dimensional environment. At the top is the canopy, a mass of leaves over 30 m above the ground. The middle layer, the understorey, is fairly open, but is criss-crossed with creepers. The ground is largely free of vegetation, because little sunlight can penetrate through the dense overhead cover.

Animal life is concentrated in and around the canopy, attracted there by the limitless supplies of food. The understorey forms a kind of internal road network. The uncluttered space allows rapid movement by birds and monkeys. The ground is largely left to insects and the forest's few large mammals.

Animal life plays a vital role in maintaining the forest. Many species carry pollen between flowers as they feed. The seeds of some trees will not germinate unless they have passed through the intestine of a particular species of monkey. Using monkeys to scatter seeds far and wide is just one of the ways the forest preserves its enormous variety of plant species.

▶ Examples of most kinds of animal live in the rain forest. Snakes, such as the Boa constrictor (1), are generally found near the forest floor, although many are excellent tree climbers. Insects are found at all levels; the Red stainer bugs (2) feed on fruit that has fallen to the ground. The coati, a small mammal (3), hunts lizards and insects, mainly on the ground. Fruit-eating bats (4) are widespread, and the Howler monkey (5), is one of the largest mammals to inhabit the canopy. Its distinctive call can be heard echoing through the forest.

35 met

15met

1

2

In the oceans

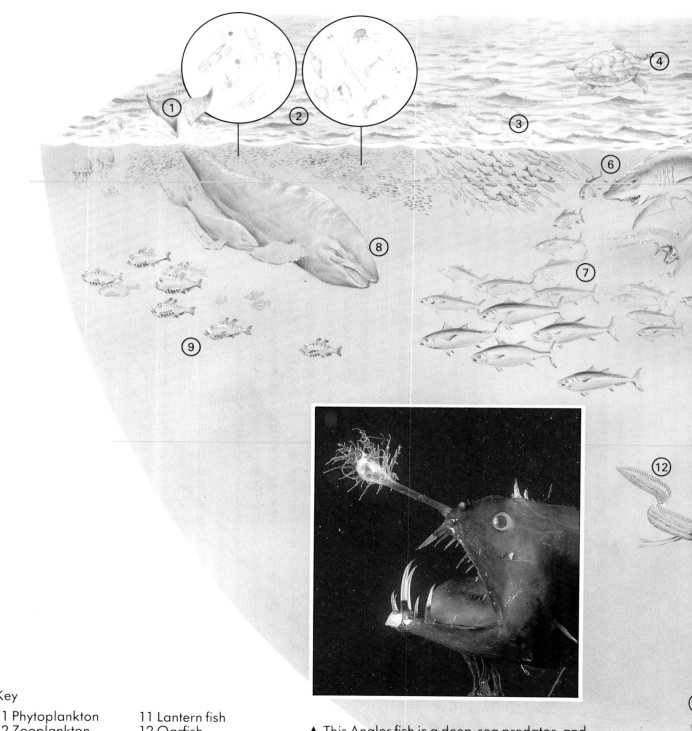

Key

1 Phytoplankton	11 Lantern fish
2 Zooplankton	12 Oarfish
3 Anchovy	13 Giant squid
4 Green turtle	14 Deep-sea jellyfish
5 Dolphin	15 Skate
6 Shark	16 Brittle star
7 Bluefin tuna	17 Deep-sea shrimp
8 Grey whale	18 Angler fish
9 Hatchet fish	19 Tripod fish
10 Squid	20 Sea cucumber

▲ This Angler fish is a deep-sea predator, and has luminous tentacles which attract smaller fish to eat in the dark waters of the ocean bottom. Food resources are scarce in the murky depths, and so most species rely on the scanty amounts of detritus (dead organic matter) that drift down from the upper layers. The Angler fish is in danger of attracting enemies with its lure as well as its prey.

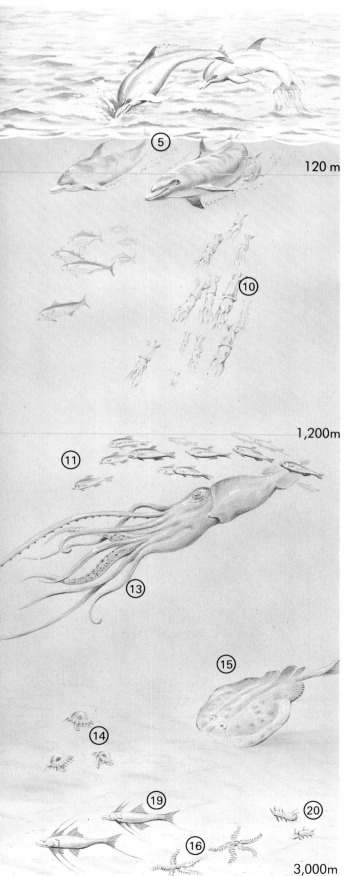

120 m

1,200m

3,000m

▲ The coral reef is a very rich habitat with thousands of species dependent on each other. At the bottom of the food web are the tiny plant plankton.

The oceans, which cover 70 per cent of the Earth's surface, contain a number of distinct ecosystems. The most productive areas are coral reefs and shallow coastal waters, where every available surface teems with life.

The ecosystem of the deep ocean falls into distinct layers. Near the surface live the microscopic plankton that are the basis of the food web. Most of the familiar species of fishes inhabit this layer, together with whales, dolphins and other aquatic mammals. Below 1,000 m, life is much scarcer because plants cannot live in the permanent darkness. Fish in this layer tend to be much smaller, although carnivores like the giant squid can grow to great size. There are also giant worms.

Plankton are the basis of life in the oceans. There are two types: microscopic plants (phytoplankton) and tiny animals (zooplankton). At the other end of the ocean's food web are the predators such as the shark, one of the top predators.

Habitats at risk

●*200,000 sq km of rain forest are destroyed every year. If this continues, the rain forest could disappear completely within the next 50 years.*

● *11 million hectares of crop-growing land are lost each year because of soil erosion. An additional 7 million hectares of grassland are lost to the gradual process of desertification.*

● *Lake Volta in Ghana, West Africa, is the world's largest artificial lake. Formed by the Akosombo Dam, it now covers 8,500 sq km of drowned land.*

▶ This lizard is one of the lucky ones being rescued by nature conservationists as its habitat is being destroyed. It lived in the area flooded by the new reservoir created by the Itaipu Dam in Brazil. There is frequently an outcry at the destruction of natural habitats during land development, but rarely can the work be halted to save them.

Our own species, *Homo sapiens sapiens*, thrives on planet Earth. Human ingenuity has enabled our population to rise way beyond any natural limits, but only at a considerable cost to nature. Our method of food production, agriculture, is not a natural process. In one sense, we are the ultimate predators, because we consume entire habitats in the struggle to feed ourselves. Sometimes we succeed only in creating wasteland which cannot be used by wildlife or ourselves.

Mining, road building, and many other human activities also threaten the balance of nature. As a result, wildlife habitats around the world are now at risk. Only concerted action, by governments, organizations and individuals, can save them.

Nature and humankind

In 1960 the world's human population reached 3,000 million; today it is over 5,000 million and still rising. This increase in numbers places enormous pressure on the planet's resources, especially for food. Each night, one in seven human beings goes to sleep hungry. Until very recently, growing more food brought us into direct conflict with natural habitats. It meant cutting down more trees and clearing more land for the plough.

For centuries, agriculture has been transforming the landscape. We first started clearing the forests over 5,000 years ago to make room for flocks and herds. Agriculture brings us into direct conflict with nature. When farming, we are imposing our own food web, with human beings at the top, on to natural ecosystems. Anything that threatens our food supplies threatens our lives. We compete with wildlife for space in which we need to grow food.

Food is not the only burden that human beings place on the environment. We are the only species with a completely unnatural lifestyle. People also need water, clothing, fuel and shelter. Half the world's timber production is burned as firewood, and the cheapest methods of extracting minerals are usually the most destructive.

Physical space is also required because people have to live somewhere, and increasingly they are moving into the wild. Sometimes the movement is bold and dramatic, as when millions of settlers move to new homes on uncleared land. But in general, there has been a slow and steady invasion of natural habitats.

▼ Human population is increasing rapidly. Every hour, 8,000 people are born. Most of the increase is taking place in tropical countries where the climate makes large-scale agriculture extremely difficult.

Using the land

Natural threats

The environment and landscapes that we know today have only appeared recently in our planet's history. They are largely the result of dramatic changes in the Earth's climate.

Many of the basic landforms were sculpted by glaciers during the last Ice Age. About 30,000 years ago, huge sheets of ice covered much of Europe and North America, and areas of forest were very much smaller. The ice-sheets began to retreat about 20,000 years ago. As they did, they uncovered huge areas of land enabling the forests to increase in size. This process is still continuing, and in Alaska, in the United States, there are spruce trees growing where there were glaciers only 200 years ago.

Ice ages are not the only form of landscaping that is beyond human control. Earthquakes, volcanoes, violent storms, even meteorites from outer space can also change the shape of the world we inhabit.

World land use

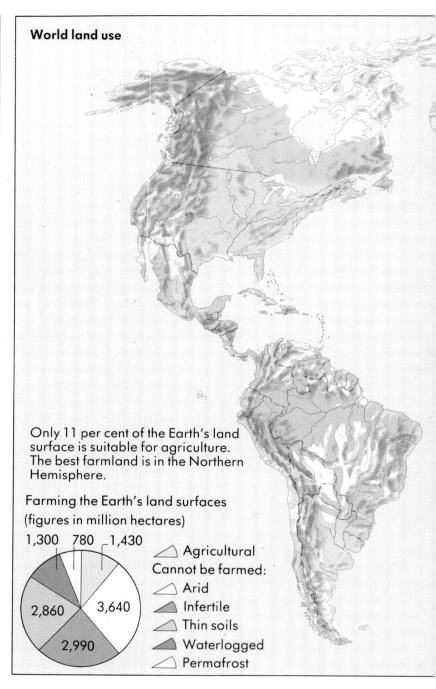

Only 11 per cent of the Earth's land surface is suitable for agriculture. The best farmland is in the Northern Hemisphere.

Farming the Earth's land surfaces
(figures in million hectares)

1,300   780   1,430

3,640

2,990

2,860

△ Agricultural
Cannot be farmed:
△ Arid
◣ Infertile
◢ Thin soils
◤ Waterlogged
△ Permafrost

Virtually all the land that is suitable for agriculture is now farmed. In the poorer countries, many people have to grow food on second-rate land that cannot sustain long-term usage. Crops become poorer every year.

Increased standards of living in the richer countries have also created greater demand for non-essentials. The result is that natural habitats are disappearing all over the world.

The northern limits of agriculture are being extended by the introduction of hybrid crops that mature during short summers. Grain fields now extend into the coniferous forest zone.

The world's temperate grasslands have long since been transformed by livestock and the plough. In the United States, there are only a few hectares of untouched prairie, which are now carefully preserved.

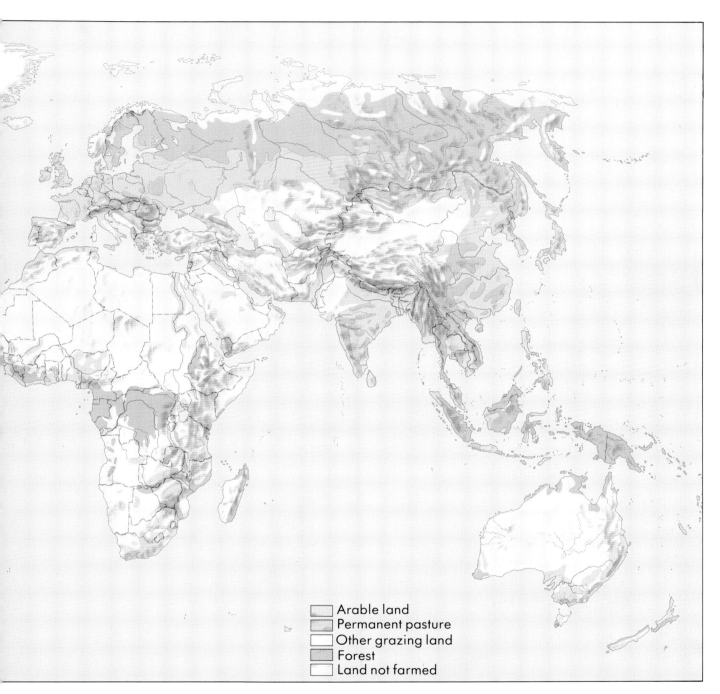

Arable land
Permanent pasture
Other grazing land
Forest
Land not farmed

In Africa, the Sahara Desert is slowly expanding southwards. The fragile ecosystem at the fringe of the desert exists in precarious balance, with uncertain rainfall. Under the weight of human numbers, and overgrazing by their flocks, the ecosystem is breaking down completely. Without plants to hold the land together, there is no barrier to the approaching sand. Not very long ago, trees covered the whole area.

Machinery greatly multiplies the destructive effects of agriculture. In Europe and North America most of the natural forests were cut down long ago. A second wave of habitat destruction is now threatening those woods, hedgerows and ponds which were unaffected by traditional farming methods. These refuges for wildlife are now being removed to create the huge fields required by modern machines.

19

Laying waste

The most dramatic example of habitat loss is the destruction of the tropical rain forests. The rain forests are disappearing at a rate of 2 per cent per year. Ranching, plantations, mining, logging and human settlement all demand their share of land. Within our lifetimes, the rain forests may disappear completely. The greatest threat to them is agriculture. In South and Central America the rain forests are being burned down to create vast cattle-ranches. Nearly all the meat produced is exported to be used in fast-food hamburger production.

This policy represents a very short-sighted use of resources which cannot be replaced. Heavy tropical rains will soon wash all the nutrients from the exposed soil. Experts predict that within 10 years, not even grass will grow where giant forest trees once stood. Once the grass dies, the soil itself will be washed away. Many scientists fear that the huge areas which have already been cleared will never regrow. The area could become a desert.

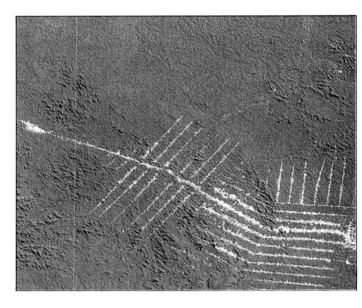

▲ The pattern of rain forest destruction in Brazil is clearly shown in this satellite image in which the vegetation shows up as red. Side roads branching off the main road give access to tree-cutting crews.

On a global scale, the rain forests represent huge masses of photosynthetic vegetation. They are responsible for recycling thousands of tonnes of carbon dioxide and oxygen every day. Without the rain forests, our atmosphere will gradually deteriorate.

Equally important is the rain forests' recycling of water. Over 75 per cent of the rain that falls on the forests is returned to the atmosphere through evaporation and plant respiration. This water may travel halfway around the globe before it falls as rain again. Perhaps a quarter of the world's human population depends on this water from the rain forests.

Preserving the rain forests is not just a matter of saving some exotic species; it might be a case of saving life on Earth.

▶ Land in Upper Egypt poisoned by excess salt (salination). Irrigating the desert is one of the chief causes of salination. As the irrigation water evaporates, it draws salt in the soil to the surface.

Unsuitable methods of agriculture can easily turn wild land into a wasteland. Natural grassland may include up to 40 different plant species. This varied mixture enables the ecosystem to flourish in regions of uncertain rainfall. There are enough drought resistant species to survive dry spells. When people plough up the grassland to create fields of a single crop, they upset the careful balance of nature. If that crop dies through drought, there is nothing to hold the soil together. It turns to dust, and may be blown or washed away.

This occurred on a large scale in the United States during the 1930s. Several years of low rainfall turned thousands of hectares of apparently good farmland into a Dust Bowl. Logging operations are also tremendously destructive, and the damage is not confined to the valuable hardwood of the rain forests. For example, it takes over 400 hectares of medium-sized coniferous trees to make a single edition of a Sunday newspaper.

◀ A landscape transformed by overgrazing in Australia. Large herds of livestock are doubly damaging. They eat all the available vegetation, and also trample plants into the ground, preventing regrowth.

Engineering the landscape

▲ Opencast china clay mine on Dartmoor, England. The local devastation caused by such mining operations is clearly apparent. In addition, mineral-laden dust may be carried great distances by the winds.

Increased human population, concentrated in rapidly expanding cities, has greatly increased demand for fuel and minerals. The Earth contains a huge range of mineral treasures. Fuels such as coal, oil and uranium, metals like aluminium and iron, and even the raw materials for concrete and glass, all have to be extracted from the ground.

Most of the mineral deposits that are readily accessible have already been exploited. The search for new supplies of fuel and metals is taking place in ever more remote areas, such as Siberia, Alaska and the Amazon Basin.

A new discovery usually spells disaster for the surrounding habitat. Humans and machines move in to tame the wilderness, felling trees and tearing up the land.

In the case of gas and oil, the greatest damage is caused by the heavy equipment used to establish the field, and with time the ecosystem can usually recover. Long-term damage, however, may be caused by pipelines carrying hot crude oil across landscapes frozen into permafrost, especially if pipes crack.

Opencast mining, employed where the mineral deposits lie just beneath the surface, is the most destructive form of exploitation. Coal, lignite, and many metal ores are commonly obtained in this manner. Huge, gaping holes are dug in to the ground, disfiguring the landscape for many years.

Mining deep underground, for coal or metals, creates the opposite problem. The surrounding area becomes dotted with unsightly slag heaps, artificial hills made of mud and crumbling stone. In the long term, both forms of mining are equally destructive because bulky minerals require roads and railways for transportation.

Roads generally mark the beginning of the end for natural habitats. They open up the land for other forms of exploitation. First the area at the roadside is cleared for firewood, then for recreation, and finally for towns and cities.

Diverting the waters

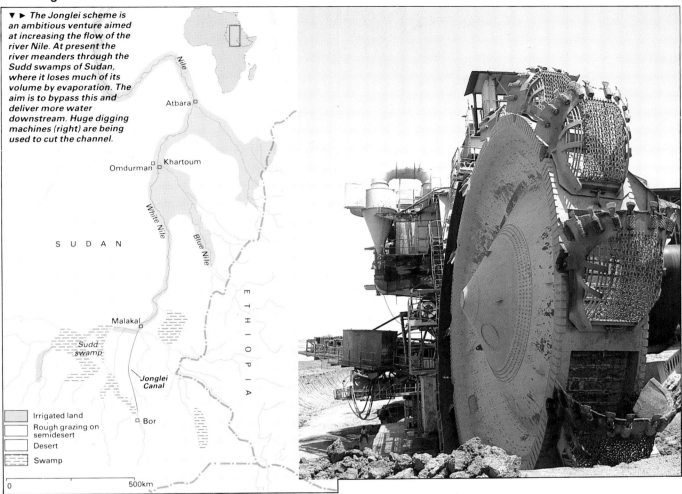

▼ ► The Jonglei scheme is an ambitious venture aimed at increasing the flow of the river Nile. At present the river meanders through the Sudd swamps of Sudan, where it loses much of its volume by evaporation. The aim is to bypass this and deliver more water downstream. Huge digging machines (right) are being used to cut the channel.

Irrigated land

Rough grazing on semidesert

Desert

Swamp

0   500km

▲ The Kariba Dam across the River Zambesi in East Africa is one of the world's largest, and was built to provide hydroelectric power.

▲ Throughout history, the most ambitious engineering schemes have been concerned with water, or hydro-engineering. There have been dams to hold back irrigation water, aqueducts to carry drinking water, and canals for transport and drainage. Today, some of the biggest machines ever built are digging the Jonglei Canal in north-east Africa. The aim is to increase the amount of water in the River Nile by diverting water from the Sudd swamps in Sudan where much of it evaporates. Huge digging machines are being used to cut a deep channel for the water. Some experts believe that the project will provide much-needed irrigation water for farmland downstream. Others fear that the canal will turn the Sudd swamps into desert.

A similar scheme in southern Russia has caused the Aral Sea, once the world's fourth largest inland sea, to lose 69 per cent of its water in less than 30 years. The shrinking of the Aral Sea has caused an ecological disaster affecting 30 million people.

Preserving the habitat

There are many organizations, at a local, national and international level, devoted to preserving the environment. Together, they form the "Green movement". In several countries there are Green political parties.

Whenever a habitat is threatened by industry or development, the Green movement takes the side of the environment. These groups already enjoy considerable public support, but their most important work is education. Unless people understand how threats to the environment affect them, they cannot appreciate the importance of preserving habitats. Every hectare that we save today is one that will be enjoyed by our grandchildren.

▼ Natural grassland, with its springtime carpet of wild flowers, is becoming rare in Europe and North America. Unless action is taken to preserve the few remaining areas, the flowers will disappear under the plough.

Many farmers are sympathetic to the Green movement, despite the pressure to grow the maximum amount of food. Some make an effort to preserve small areas of woodland and hedgerow, and are careful not to spray these areas with pesticides. A few have turned their backs on modern methods and use no chemicals at all, either in fertilizers or pesticides.

Farming without chemicals is known as organic farming. In many countries, organic produce has become very popular. Because no chemicals are used to grow the food, there are none to enter the human food chain. In addition, by choosing organic produce, people are also choosing to save the countryside.

In the developing countries, action is finally being taken to save the rain forests. In Africa, the Ivory Coast has recently banned all timber exports. In Central America, the government of Panama has made it illegal to cut down any tree more than five years old. Such actions show great determination, because timber exports have been a major source of income.

It is difficult to persuade poor people in developing countries of the importance of saving the forests. They need more food and want to use the land to grow it on. But saving habitats is not a luxury, it is a necessity. What is at stake is not just our enjoyment of nature, but the future of life on Earth.

◄ Wicken Fen Nature Reserve in England. Wetlands, such as marshes and bogs, are extremely rich in rare plant and animal species. Unfortunately, they also make excellent farmland after they have been drained.

▼ Yellowstone National Park in the United States, famous for its Grizzly bears and spectacular geysers. Most countries have established National Parks where wildlife is protected and development is prohibited.

Species at risk

▶ The Golden lion tamarin is a small monkey and now very rare in the wild. It lives only in forest remnants in eastern Brazil. Hundreds have been exported for zoos and for the pet trade. This is now illegal, but still continues. Their habitat is almost completely destroyed by development for the tourist trade.

When a species becomes extinct, it disappears for ever. Extinction is a natural part of evolution, but it is usually a slow process. Human beings speed things up. Some animals that are known from photographs taken during the last century are now extinct. Today, a huge international trade in animals and animal products is consuming the planet's wildlife. We are also destroying the habitats in which they live. Directly or indirectly, human activity now threatens many familiar species. Yet it is only through our intervention that many endangered species have any chance of survival at all. On the other hand, some wildlife species thrive in human company, but these are often the least welcome.

Animal products

Human beings have an insatiable appetite for animal protein. In China, where almost everything is considered edible, the wildlife is steadily being eaten to extinction. The world's oceans are under similar threat. Overfishing can cause dramatic changes in the size of marine populations. In 1937 California landed 750,000 tonnes of sardines; by 1957 this had fallen to a mere 17 tonnes. Such a rapid decrease in numbers creates a gap in natural food chains that can affect other species.

At the beginning of the last century, there were perhaps 40 million bison roaming the North American prairies. By 1900, only 500 remained. The vast majority of those slaughtered were left to rot. The hunters only wanted the hides for leather.

Many other species have been hunted to the point of extinction for their skins and furs. Countless beavers, otters, seals, minks, bears, leopards and other big cats have been sacrificed in the name of fashion and status. Human fancies have created an international trade in animal products: exotic feathers for hats, turtle shells for combs, and recently the craze for rare and exotic pets.

Easy money is the motive. The poachers become rich, while the world becomes poorer. Several species of rhinoceros have disappeared because their horns were thought to have magic powers. Today, the African elephant is being wiped out for the sake of its tusks. The ivory is considered valuable because it can be carved into souvenirs for tourists.

◀ These African zebra skins may be destined to upholster prestige furniture in Europe or North America. Most of the demand for furs and skins comes from the developed countries which have destroyed nearly all their own wildlife. Animal products are a valuable export commodity for many developing countries.

▼ These ivory carvings are made from the tusks of the African elephant. The population of African elephant is dropping very quickly, largely because of ivory poaching. Poaching gangs operate in game reserves despite armed patrols. These carvings were seized by customs as ivory exports are illegal.

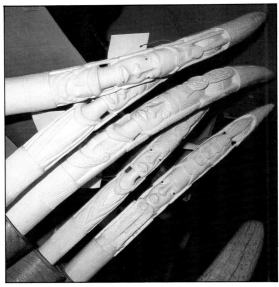

The march of extinction

1 Mammoth
2 Woolly rhinoceros
3 Cave lion
4 Cave bear
5 Irish elk
6 American mastodon
7 Imperial mammoth
8 Giant ground sloth
9 Saber-tooth "tiger"
10 Dire wolf
11 Reunion solitaire
12 Dodo
13 Guadaloupe amazon
14 Elephant bird
15 Auroch
16 Steller's sea cow
17 Blue buck
18 Hispaniolan hutia
19 Green and yellow macaw

20 Moa
21 Dwarf emu
22 Rodriguez little owl
23 Sandwich rail
24 Great auk
25 Spectacled cormorant
26 Atlas bear
27 Tarpan
28 Sea mink
29 Portuguese ibex
30 Quagga
31 Warrah
32 Palestine painted frog
33 Abingdon Island tortoise
34 Round Island boa
35 Passenger pigeon
36 Carolina parakeet
37 Pink-headed duck
38 Lord Howe Island white eye

39 Hawaiian O-O
40 Madagascar serpent eagle
41 Kauai Nukupuu
42 Greater rabbit bandicoot
43 Arizona jaguar
44 Schomburgk's deer
45 Caribbean monk seal
46 Thylacine "wolf"
47 Jamaican long-tongued bat
48 Barbary lion
49 Newfoundland white wolf
50 Bali tiger
51 Italian spade-footed toad
52 Chinese alligator
53 Central Asian cobra
54 Geometric tortoise
55 Hawksbill turtle
56 Japanese crested ibis
57 California condor

58 Red-billed curassow
59 Black robin
60 Reunion petrel
61 Abbott's booby
62 Hawaiian gallinule
63 Mauritius pink pigeon
64 Western ground parrot
65 Hawaiian crow
66 Leadbeater's oppossum
67 Ghost bat
68 Woolly spider monkey
69 Mountain gorilla
70 Blue whale
71 Humpback whale
72 Indus dolphin
73 Northern kit fox
74 Baluchistan bear
75 Giant otter
76 Siberian tiger

77 Asiatic lion
78 Mediterranean monk seal
79 Grevy's zebra
80 Przewalski's horse
81 Mountain tapir
82 Great Indian rhinoceros
83 Swamp deer
84 Giant sable antelope
85 Indri
86 Orangutan
87 Sumatran rhinoceros
88 Mountain anoa

Extinct and endangered species

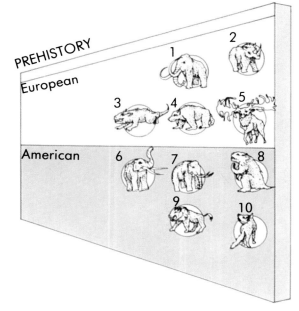

Recently-discovered evidence suggests that early humans played an important role in the extinction of some prehistoric animals. During the last 500 years, people have certainly left their mark on the world's wildlife. Dozens of species known to our ancestors have now vanished. Only pictures and descriptions remain. Species that live in islands are more vulnerable than those on the mainland.

Perhaps the most frightening example is the North American Passenger pigeon. During the early 1800s, a single flock was estimated to contain over 2,000 million individuals. Through a combination of habitat destruction and hunting for food and sport, the bird had disappeared from the wild by the end of the century. The last ever Passenger pigeon died in a zoo in 1914.

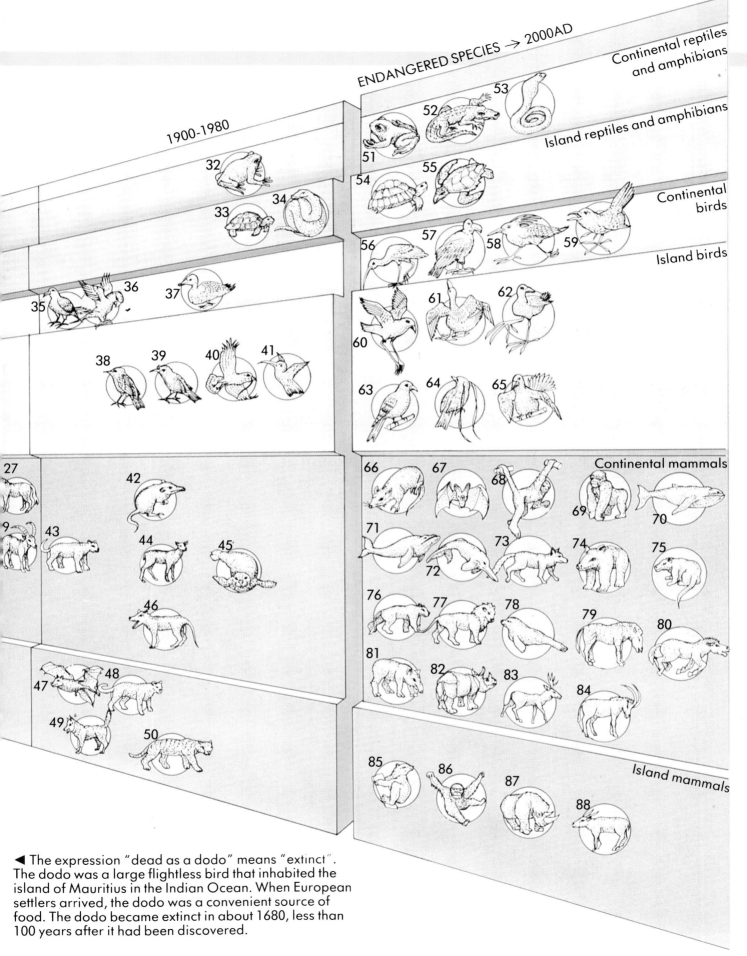

1900-1980

Continental reptiles and amphibians

Island reptiles and amphibians

Continental birds

Island birds

Continental mammals

Island mammals

◄ The expression "dead as a dodo" means "extinct". The dodo was a large flightless bird that inhabited the island of Mauritius in the Indian Ocean. When European settlers arrived, the dodo was a convenient source of food. The dodo became extinct in about 1680, less than 100 years after it had been discovered.

On the edge

Today, some of the world's most familiar animal species stand at the edge of extinction. Over 6,000 species are officially acknowledged to be endangered, and the list is far from complete. Large animals are especially at risk from habitat destruction. Their natural populations tend to be quite small, because each individual requires proportionately more territory.

The African elephant is the world's largest land animal. During the last ten years, its numbers have been halved from 1.3 million to 600,000, by ivory poachers. Its smaller cousin, the Asiatic or Indian elephant, is reduced to about 30,000 individuals living in the wild.

Survival at sea
In the oceans, the aquatic mammals are perhaps most at risk. Twelve species of whale are endangered, and the Grey whale has only been saved from extinction by 50 years of international protection. The one remaining species of dugong, or sea-cow, is still being hunted in Indonesia. In the Mediterranean, the Monk seal population is now less than 1,000.

Nor are human beings especially careful about their own close relatives. There are at least 50 species of primate in danger. The gorillas and the orang-utans now exist only in very small numbers. Declining chimpanzee populations are causing concern throughout Africa. Many small animal species, such as the Golden marmoset, are now seriously threatened by the growing demand for exotic pets.

Many extinctions have been caused by humans introducing animal predators. For the last 50 years, no offspring of one species of giant Galapagos tortoise have survived. The young are eaten by black rats which arrived on the Galapagos Islands with human settlers. Other unique island species are also under threat. In Madagascar, populations of some rare primates such as aye-ayes and lemurs number less than 100 individuals.

▶ The Giant panda is found only in a small area of southern China. There are about 200 pandas left in the wild, and they very rarely breed in captivity. When the last wild panda dies, extinction will surely follow.

▲ The shy and gentle Mountain gorilla is one of the world's rarest animals. Its habitat in West Africa is disappearing under the pressure of human cultivation. Tourists who are drawn to these remote areas to see wild gorillas are increasingly damaging the habitat.

◄ The Southern Right whale is one of the world's largest living animals. Formerly killed in large numbers, they are now "commercially extinct". This means that it is not worth the expense of hunting the last few. This has extended the species' life a little, but there may not be enough individuals left for the population to recover.

Saving species

◄ Przewalski's horse now exists only in captivity, but in sizeable numbers. Zoologists would like to release some back into Central Asia, but they are concerned that it has become adapted to life in zoos.

► The White rhinoceros, like all rhinoceros species, is seriously endangered. In 1979 Project Rhino was launched to coordinate attempts to save them. Poachers are still a deadly threat to rhinoceroses.

▼ The Arabian oryx became extinct in the wild in 1972. Fortunately, Operation Oryx had already established a small herd in an American zoo, which bred success-fully. During the late 1970s the oryx was released back to the wild.

Perhaps the most important thing we can do for endangered species is to recognize their plight. Publicity from concerned governments, and organizations such as the World Wide Fund for Nature (WWF), have done a great deal to raise public awareness. Intervening to solve the problem, however, is very difficult.

Zoos provide endangered species with a mixed blessing. Although care may be given them in captivity, the methods of capture are not always so gentle. The normal way of "taking" a young mammal is to first kill its mother. With tropical birds, as many as 50 may be killed for every live specimen taken.

Game reserves, which protect animals and their natural habitat, are much more humane. But the habitat may be too inaccessible, and there is the problem of providing armed guards. Many poachers will start a gun battle with the game wardens rather than be caught.

If the species will breed in zoos, there is hope that a population may eventually be released back to the wild. Some species, however, do not breed in captivity. In a few cases, entire wild populations have been carefully collected, and then transported to a less threatened habitat. Sometimes they have been released on to a game reserve, but for others a remote island has offered the only chance of safety. But there are fewer and fewer wild places left where animals can be safe from our exploitation of the land.

In many parts of the world, governments and international organizations have successfully cooperated to protect endangered wildlife. A series of projects has given several species a fighting chance of survival. At the other end of the scale, important work is also done by small local groups devoted to saving a single plant or insect species. One of the most important lessons of ecology is that every species has its role to play in the balance of nature, and therefore every species is important.

Project Tiger

The Bali and Caspian tigers are now extinct. The Siberian and Javan tigers are unlikely to survive the century outside zoos. The Bengal tiger is the only species that is likely to survive in the wild. Project Tiger is the master-plan for saving the Bengal tigers.

The Indian government, with support from the WWF, has established nine tiger reserves. Trained rangers and armed guards protect the animals against poachers and forest fires. Some animals are fitted with electronic collars to monitor their movements.

Thriving with people

Representatives of several animal groups – mammals, birds and insects – have adapted to human existence so well that they have become pests. Most of them have completely abandoned a wild existence, and have become parasites on human food webs. From the time people began sailing the world, they travelled around the globe in ships' cargoes. These species now live near people all over the world.

There are over 3,500 known species of cockroach. A few of these have become such close companions of people that "roaches" are now almost universally despised. Able to eat virtually anything, and resistant to insecticides, cockroaches spoil human food and spread disease. The Oriental and German cockroaches have become a familiar sight in millions of homes around the world.

The House mouse originated in Central Asia, but has spread around the world. The species has found a niche in the nooks and crannies of human habitations. Maintaining a cautious and nocturnal existence, mice scavenge food from human stores and waste. Its larger cousins, the Brown and Black rats, are far more destructive. Both rat and mice populations can undergo very rapid growth when conditions are good. These pests can consume huge quantities of stored food in homes and warehouses.

Larger woodland mammals are slowly coming to terms with humans, and the process is speeded up by the growth of suburbs. Racoons or foxes are quite a common sight in country gardens, and both species are now adapting to life in the city. In parts of Alaska, Polar bears are known to raid dustbins.

Common racoon

Black-headed gull

Herring gull

House mouse

Norway rat

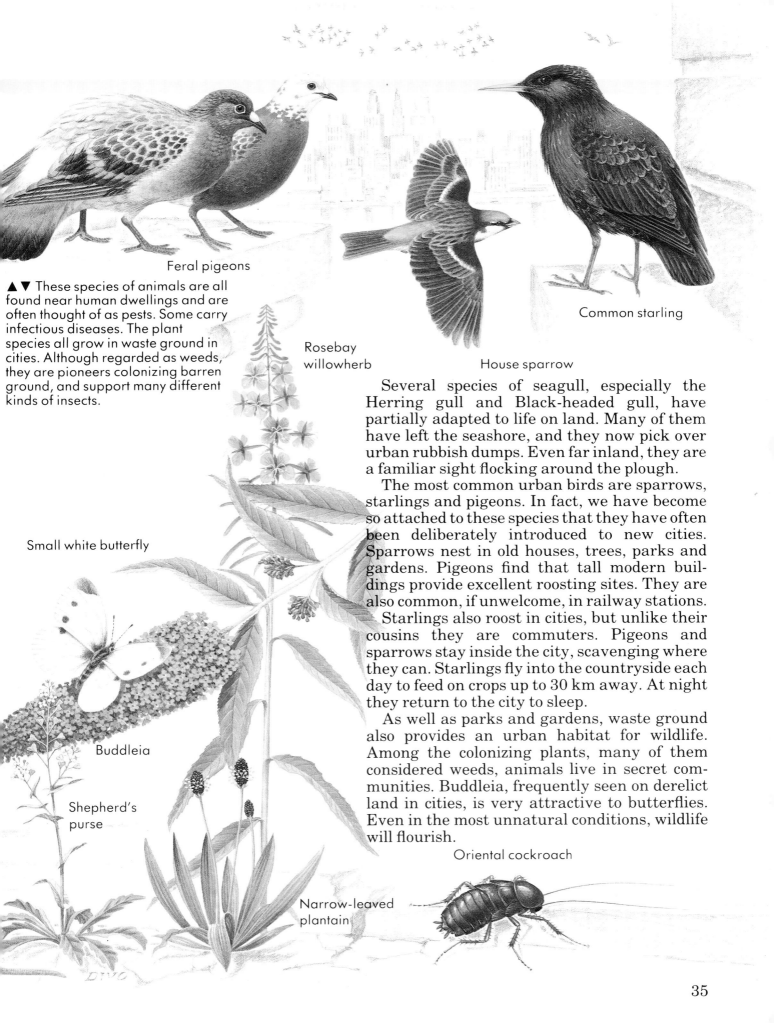

Feral pigeons

Common starling

House sparrow

Rosebay willowherb

▲▼ These species of animals are all found near human dwellings and are often thought of as pests. Some carry infectious diseases. The plant species all grow in waste ground in cities. Although regarded as weeds, they are pioneers colonizing barren ground, and support many different kinds of insects.

Small white butterfly

Buddleia

Shepherd's purse

Narrow-leaved plantain

Oriental cockroach

Several species of seagull, especially the Herring gull and Black-headed gull, have partially adapted to life on land. Many of them have left the seashore, and they now pick over urban rubbish dumps. Even far inland, they are a familiar sight flocking around the plough.

The most common urban birds are sparrows, starlings and pigeons. In fact, we have become so attached to these species that they have often been deliberately introduced to new cities. Sparrows nest in old houses, trees, parks and gardens. Pigeons find that tall modern buildings provide excellent roosting sites. They are also common, if unwelcome, in railway stations.

Starlings also roost in cities, but unlike their cousins they are commuters. Pigeons and sparrows stay inside the city, scavenging where they can. Starlings fly into the countryside each day to feed on crops up to 30 km away. At night they return to the city to sleep.

As well as parks and gardens, waste ground also provides an urban habitat for wildlife. Among the colonizing plants, many of them considered weeds, animals live in secret communities. Buddleia, frequently seen on derelict land in cities, is very attractive to butterflies. Even in the most unnatural conditions, wildlife will flourish.

Pollution

Spot facts

• 110 million tonnes a year of sulphur dioxide (a major cause of acid rain) are released into the atmosphere.

• Over 8,000 different pollutants have been identified in water taken from lakes.

• Cleaning up after the nuclear accident at Three Mile Island in the USA will cost over $1,000 million.

• Pollution travels. Acidic chemicals can be carried 2,000 km by the wind before falling to Earth as acid rain.

• 800 years ago King Edward I of England imposed a death penalty on anyone found burning coal because it created noxious fumes.

▶ This Western grebe is being cleaned of the sticky crude oil which prevents it flying and feeding. The oil spilled accidentally into the San Francisco Bay, USA, from a Standard Oil tanker. Emergency bird-cleaning teams can help rescue some seabirds after a large disaster such as this. Pollution of the sea, lakes and rivers causes untold damage to wildlife.

Human beings are the only species that poison their own habitat. If we think of our planet as a spaceship, then we are the crew and all the other species are passengers. In general, we behave like hooligans, strewing the communal living-quarters with rubbish. Earth's atmosphere forms a protective cocoon around our spaceship, which uses it to store and recycle essential elements such as carbon and oxygen. Humans fill the air with pollution that turns the rain acidic, and threatens to alter the climate.

Pollution from fossil and nuclear fuels, from industry and agriculture, are slowly poisoning the land, air and water that we share with all living things.

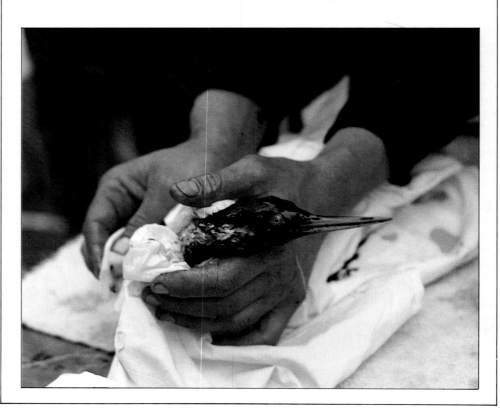

Poisoning the world

▲ Workers in protective clothing and masks clearing up after an explosion at a pesticide factory in Seveso, Italy. The ingredients of pesticides include some of the most poisonous chemicals we know.

◄ Mountains of solid waste disfigure the landscape. Little grows here. Metal and paper will eventually rust and rot, but some of the plastic will last for many years before it eventually decomposes.

All living organisms produce waste products. With all species except humans, these are safely recycled by the ecosphere. We alone produce unnatural waste, and we produce it in huge quantities. Atmospheric pollution began when human beings first discovered fire, but for thousands of years it had little impact on the environment. Serious problems started during the 1800s with the coal-burning factories of the Industrial Revolution. The smoke belching from their chimneys turned buildings and trees black with soot. Today, factory smoke is much "cleaner". The black soot has largely been eliminated, but invisible combustion products continue to pour into the air.

In the 1900s, huge numbers of motor vehicles have greatly increased the burden on the atmosphere. Vehicle exhaust fumes contain several harmful substances. These include carbon monoxide, a highly poisonous gas, nitrogen oxide, which produces acid rain; and lead, which is deadly to most forms of life. The volume of motor traffic is steadily increasing.

Industry is responsible for a wide range of other pollutants. Many of the chemicals used in industry are poisonous, and others are known to cause cancer or deformities in babies. In many countries, especially in recent years, industry is very careful, but accidents do happen. A single chemical spillage can cause a river to become lifeless for years. Some companies have disposed of their waste chemicals by dumping them on empty land. This land is now completely uninhabitable.

Most modern farmers use large quantities of powerful chemicals to kill weeds and insects. Even in the dilute concentrations used in spraying, these can damage wildlife.

Some of these chemicals tend to accumulate in animals' bodies. The insecticide DDT is a notorious example. When such a chemical enters the food chain, it gets passed along. The higher up the food chain an animal is, the more chemicals it absorbs. This process is known as bio-concentration. Predators, such as birds of prey, are especially at risk.

Polluting the air

Each year millions of tonnes of pollution from power stations, factories and motor vehicles enters the atmosphere. Most countries have agreed to reduce the pollution caused by industry. Some now require motor vehicles to be fitted with devices to filter out pollutants, or to use cleaner types of petrol.

Despite these measures, the effects of atmospheric pollution are often felt below. Acid rain is created when the products of burning coal and oil, combustion products, become combined with water in the atmosphere to form acids. Falling back to Earth as rain, these acids directly attack trees and plants. Acidic water also accumulates in rivers and lakes, killing fish and other aquatic life. The acid destroys the natural chemical balance.

In Britain, over 60 per cent of the forests have been harmed by acid rain, and large areas of North America are similarly affected. The winds often take acid rain to neighbouring countries. Southern Norway, for example, has few heavy factories, yet 80 per cent of its lakes are now devoid of life or on the critical list.

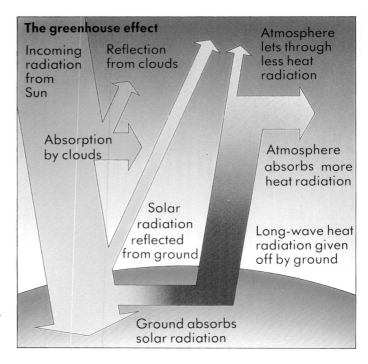

The greenhouse effect

Incoming radiation from Sun

Reflection from clouds

Atmosphere lets through less heat radiation

Absorption by clouds

Solar radiation reflected from ground

Atmosphere absorbs more heat radiation

Long-wave heat radiation given off by ground

Ground absorbs solar radiation

▲ Carbon dioxide has formed a blanket around the planet. Heat energy from the Sun is trapped by the atmosphere, which is slowly warming up.

Bhopal

Accidental air pollution by industrial chemicals can have disastrous local effects.

On 3 December 1984, there was an accident at a pesticide factory in the town of Bhopal, India. An explosion released 30 tonnes of methyl isocyanate, a highly toxic gas, into the air. Over 200,000 people in the vicinity were exposed to the gas. About 2,500 people were killed immediately, as many as 10,000 may have died subsequently, and at least 20,000 were disabled for life.

The Bhopal incident drew attention to one of the most important pollution issues. The rich countries of Europe and North America can afford to be concerned about pollution. They have well-developed industrial economies, and can impose high standards of safety and cleanliness. Poorer countries in the developing world often cannot afford to take these measures, even though they may wish to.

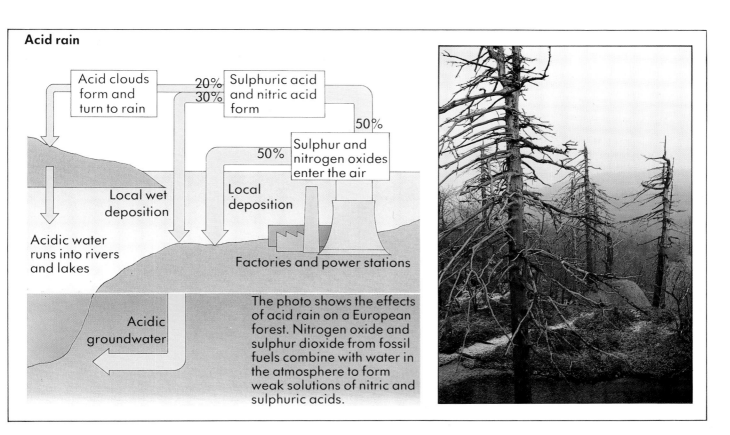

Acid rain

Acid clouds form and turn to rain

20%
30%

Sulphuric acid and nitric acid form

50%

50%

Sulphur and nitrogen oxides enter the air

Local wet deposition

Local deposition

Acidic water runs into rivers and lakes

Factories and power stations

Acidic groundwater

The photo shows the effects of acid rain on a European forest. Nitrogen oxide and sulphur dioxide from fossil fuels combine with water in the atmosphere to form weak solutions of nitric and sulphuric acids.

Human activity is producing far more carbon dioxide gas than the oceans and forests can recycle. On a global scale, increased amounts of carbon dioxide in the atmosphere threaten to change the climate of the whole planet. As the gas accumulates in the upper atmosphere it creates an insulating layer around the planet. Scientists believe that average temperatures on Earth might rise by 4°C. The ice caps could melt and many countries be flooded by rising seas.

This problem is often called the greenhouse effect. Carbon dioxide from burning fuel is the main culprit, but other gases are also involved. The propellant gases in many aerosols, chlorofluorocarbons (CFCs) are especially damaging to the atmosphere. As well as adding to the greenhouse effect, CFCs are also dissolving the Earth's ozone layer. Without ozone to act as a filter, the Sun's rays can be harmful to living things.

◀ Smog over Mexico City. Fumes from the burning of fossil fuels can become trapped near the ground by a layer of air. The action of sunlight on the trapped fumes produces a poisonous smog.

Nuclear hazards

Radioactivity occurs naturally: many rocks are slightly radioactive. As life on Earth evolved, it adapted to this background radiation. Humans first discovered the secrets of atomic and nuclear power in the 1940s. Since then, pollution from unnatural radioactivity has become a potential health hazard. There has been considerable debate about what constitutes a safe dose of radiation. Today, most scientists agree that any exposure to unnatural radiation is dangerous, and a risk not worth taking.

The world's first exposure to radiation pollution followed the use and testing of atomic weapons. Nearly 1,500 bombs have been detonated, most of them in the atmosphere, although the earliest tests were made in deserts and on remote islands. These explosions have scattered tonnes of radioactive fall-out around the world. Some of the fall-out loses its radiation within a short time. But some of the radioactive substances, or radioisotopes, remain dangerous for many years.

These isotopes enter food chains via plants, and can accumulate in animal bodies and be passed along food chains. In the past there was considerable concern about the amount of the isotope strontium-90 in cows' milk. International agreement has now almost put an end to atomic tests.

Today, the use of nuclear power to generate electricity is the main focus of concern. Although nuclear power stations are designed to be as safe as possible, there is always some leakage of radiation during operation. There is also the problem of what to do with the radioactive fuel after use. Additionally, there is always the possibility of an accident.

▼ The nuclear power station at Three Mile Island, Pennsylvania, USA, has been shut down since the accident there on 28 March 1979. Mechanical failure caused the reactor to overheat, which might have led to a far greater catastrophe. After 18 hours, engineers were able to bring the reactor under control and so averted the danger of a deadly explosion.

There have been two major accidents at nuclear power stations. In 1979, a pump failed at the Three Mile Island installation in the United States. The operators managed to prevent an explosion, but the power station was wrecked and a considerable amount of radiation was released into the atmosphere.

In 1986, their Russian counterparts were not so successful, and the Chernobyl power station exploded. The explosion produced a cloud of fall-out that spread over 75 per cent of Europe. Even in Sweden, thousands of kilometres from Chernobyl, livestock had to be kept under cover to protect it from the fall-out. Experts predict that at least 1,000 people in Western Europe will eventually die as a result of eating food contaminated by the fall-out from Chernobyl.

These two accidents have caused many people, and some governments, to have second thoughts about nuclear power. There will always be a risk, and the next accident might be much worse.

▲ Checking vegetables with a Geiger counter, which measures radioactivity. Meat and milk products gave the most concern after Chernobyl. In Britain, a ban was put on the sale of sheep from areas that received the heaviest fall-out. Over 500 farms were still affected a year later.

◀ When the nuclear reactor at Chernobyl exploded in 1986, it blew apart the entire building and started a fire. Some of the first casualties were firemen who received fatal doses of radiation while bravely fighting the blaze. At least 200 Russians have so far died as a result of the explosion, and many towns and villages have been permanently evacuated.

Polluting the waters

All the waters of the Earth are bombarded with pollutants. Rain and rivers wash our waste into lakes and seas where it slowly accumulates. Natural processes can remove some, but by no means all, of the pollutants that household and industrial waste contains.

In Europe, the River Rhine alone carries over 300,000 tonnes of waste into the North Sea each year. Most of this is permitted waste: sewage and waste chemicals that most scientists believe the sea can safely absorb. But a series of accidents have also spilled many tonnes of highly poisonous substances.

Cities and industry are not the only cause of water pollution. The artificial fertilizers that many farmers depend on can also pollute water supplies. The phosphates and nitrates contained in artificial fertilizer are easily washed out of the soil by rain. These nutrient chemicals accumulate in rivers and lakes, where they destroy the natural balance of nutrients.

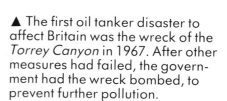

▲ The first oil tanker disaster to affect Britain was the wreck of the *Torrey Canyon* in 1967. After other measures had failed, the government had the wreck bombed, to prevent further pollution.

▲ (Inset) In 1978 an oil spillage from the tanker *Amoco Cadiz* devastated part of the French coastline. A national emergency was declared, and cleaning up operations lasted for months.

◄ Several countries continue to pump chemical wastes and untreated sewage into the sea. Many beaches have been declared unfit for swimming because of the potential health risks from this pollution.

The increased concentrations of nutrients stimulate algae (microscopic waterplants) to overgrow. When the nutrient resouces are all used up, the algae die. As they decompose, all the oxygen in the water is used up and the environment becomes lifeless.

This process, which is known as eutrophication, usually occurs in small bodies of water. Recently, however, it has been blamed for the great masses of dead algae that have been observed in some of the world's smaller seas.

Enclosed seas, such as the Mediterranean Sea and the Baltic Sea, are particularly at risk from water pollution. Their coasts are lined with industry, and they have only narrow outlets into the main oceans. Pollution therefore becomes more concentrated, and the effects on marine life are much greater. These seas may soon become completely dead.

Oil is probably Earth's most valuable and useful commodity, and hundreds of millions of tonnes are carried by tanker each year. Inevitably there have been accidents, and large quantities of crude oil have spilled into the sea.

Crude oil floats on the surface, and decomposes in a few weeks under the action of seawater and sunlight. When the spillage occurs close to land, and oil is washed ashore, a few weeks is far too long. The oil coats everything and has a disastrous effect on the local ecosystem. Seabirds and aquatic mammals sink and drown, shellfish are smothered, and many fish are poisoned.

Water pollution has spread to the poles, and has now entered the Antarctic food chains. The choice is quite simple: either we clean up, and halt the steady increase in pollution, or our planet will slowly die.

Glossary

acid rain Rainwater containing pollutants that chemically attacks stone and trees, and which can rapidly make a river or lake completely lifeless.

adaptation Process by which the characteristics of a species gradually change in response to the environment. The term can also refer to a particular characteristic.

bacteria Group of microorganisms that are neither plants nor animals. They are the smallest and most primitive form of life. A few species cause disease in humans and are a major pest.

bio-concentration Process by which a pollutant is retained inside animal bodies, and becomes more concentrated as it moves up a food chain.

canopy Layer of dense foliage that forms the roof of a rain forest about 30 m above the ground. It is the most densely populated part of the forest.

carbon dioxide Gas present in Earth's atmosphere that is essential to many of the processes of life. Increased levels of carbon dioxide, caused by pollution and habitat destruction, are slowly causing our planet to get warmer.

carnivore Animal that feeds on other animals; a meat-eater.

CFCs Group of gases widely used as aerosol propellants that are believed to be causing considerable damage to the Earth's ozone layer.

climax community End product of the process of succession; a community composed of long-established populations living in a natural balance with each other.

colonists Species that have adaptations that enable them to establish themselves on any unoccupied land that becomes available.

combustion products Fumes and minute particles released into the atmosphere during the process of combustion (burning).

community All the plants and animals that exist within a shared habitat. Communities are the building blocks from which ecosystems are constructed.

detritus Silt and sediment that usually contains dead and decaying organic matter.

ecology Study of the relationships between living organisms and their environment. Ecologists look at the bigger picture, the way species behave towards each other.

ecosphere Planet Earth. Our planet is the only object in the Universe on which we know life exists. We only have one ecosphere available for study.

ecosystem Network of relationships between species living in a particular location. An ecosystem can be as large as an ocean, or as small as a single field.

endangered Describes a species that because of decreasing population or shrinking habitat, (or a combination of both), is likely to become extinct in the wild unless it is carefully protected.

environment All physical conditions, e.g. land surface (or type of water), climate, atmosphere and other life forms, that together form the normal surroundings for a particular species.

eutrophication Process by which the oxygen in a body of water becomes used up by the decaying bodies of microorganisms that were stimulated into overgrowth by an abundance of nutrients. A common result of nitrate pollution.

evolution Generally accepted theory that life on Earth began in very simple forms that have slowly developed into the more complex forms.

fall-out Fine dust of radioactive particles produced by the explosion of a nuclear device on the Earth's surface, or in the atmosphere.

fertilization The first stage of sexual reproduction, in which a male sex cell and a female sex cell join together to form a single cell that will develop into a new individual.

food chain Process by which many animals that eat food, in turn become food for others e.g. cows eat grass, people eat cows. Food chains indicate a flow of energy through an ecosystem towards the top predators.

food web Map of the movement of food (energy) through an ecosystem. Food webs are usually pyramid-shaped, with predators at the top.

fungi Group of organisms, including mushrooms and moulds, that share a few of the characteristics of primitive plants, but which do not photosynthesize.

game reserve Protected area within which wildlife can enjoy an almost natural existence.

glaciation Process by which the land surface is smoothed and shaped by the action of glaciers, rivers of ice that move very slowly. Today, glaciers are confined to mountainous regions and the poles.

greenhouse effect Gradual warming of the Earth's atmosphere due to pollution, mainly in the form of carbon dioxide.

Green movement Unofficial alliance of many different pressure groups who are concerned with various environmental and ecological issues such as preserving habitats and wildlife, and preventing pollution.

habitat Natural surroundings in which a particular plant or animal exists. The term is much more specific and localized than "environment".

herbivore Animal that feeds exclusively on plants.

Industrial Revolution Period of rapid industrial development that occurred in Britain during the 1800s, characterized by a massive increase in the use of coal as a fuel.

national park Area of land within which building or development is not permitted, and the wildlife is strictly protected.

niche Position of a species within an ecosystem, defined by the space the species occupies, and by its feeding activity.

nitrate Chemical compound containing the element nitrogen, the main ingredient of artificial fertilizers.

nuclear Relating to the nucleus, or central part of an atom. Nuclear energy is the energy produced when atoms, particularly uranium atoms, split.

omnivore Animal that feeds on both plant and vegetable matter. Omniverous species, e.g. humans, rats, cockroaches, are among the most successful.

organic farming Any method of cultivating food that does not involve the use of chemical additives such as pesticides or artificial fertilizer.

ozone Form of oxygen gas, the "tang" in sea air. A layer of ozone near the top of the atmosphere filters out most of the harmful effects of the sun's rays.

parasites Organisms that obtain nourishment by feeding directly off the body systems of others. Livestock are liable to infestation with both external parasites (ticks and fleas) and internal parasites (flukes and worms).

pesticide Substance that kills pests. Some use natural ingredients, but most contain poisonous synthetic chemicals that can become concentrated in natural food chains.

plankton Tiny, single-celled plants and animals that live in both salt and fresh water. Plant plankton, also known as phytoplankton, form the basis for most of the ocean's food web, and, like land plants, remove carbon dioxide from the atmosphere.

phosphate Chemical compound containing the element phosphorous, one of the main ingredients of artificial fertilizer.

pollen Tiny grains produced by flowers that contain the plant's male sex cells.

pollution Introduction and distribution of unnatural amounts of many different and dangerous substances into the land, water and air that form our environment.

pollutant Any substance that is present in the environment in unnatural quantities, whether it is directly harmful or not.

population All the members of a particular species that exist within a defined area. In nature, populations rise and fall in relation to the availability of food.

predator Any animal that actively hunts other animals (known as prey) for food. Most carnivores are also predators.

photosynthesis Process by which plants manufacture food from carbon dioxide, water and sunlight.

primary consumers Animals that feed on plants (primary producers).

primary producers Plants, so-called because of the role they play in food webs, producing food by photosynthesis.

rain forest Extremely lush and diverse form of natural vegetation that mainly occurs in tropical regions. The rain forests contain at least half of all species on Earth, and are also vital to the proper functioning of the atmosphere.

radiation Means by which energy travels through empty space or a gas, e.g. the atmosphere. The term is widely used to refer to the energy produced by radioactivity.

radioactivity Property of some naturally occuring and synthetic substances to spontaneously emit energy which is harmful to life in anything but very small doses.

radioisotope Radioactive form of an element; carbon-14 is a radioisotope of carbon.

secondary consumers Meat-eaters (carnivores), so-called because the energy they receive from food has already been processed by primary consumers (herbivores).

smog Form of localized atmospheric pollution that occurs over some large cities. The action of sunlight on vehicle exhaust fumes creates a thick layer of dirty and often poisonous air.

soil erosion Loss of topsoil (the most fertile layer) through the action of wind and water.

species The most precise form of grouping of a type of plant or animal. All members of the same species have the same characteristics and differ only slightly in size or markings. Breeding does not take place between species.

succession Process by which an area of new or cleared ground is occupied by a series of species. Fast-growing plants with windborne seeds are usually the first species to establish themselves.

understorey Layer of relatively open space that occurs inside rain forests, between the forest floor and the dense foliage of the tree-tops (the canopy).

zooplankton Minute aquatic animals, food for the smallest of the underwater predators.

Index

Further Reading

Alternative Energy series (Wayland)
Atlas of the Living World by David Attenborough (Weidenfeld and Nicholson, 1989)
The Blue Peter Green Book by Lewis Bronze, Nick Heathcote and Peter Brown (BBC Books/Sainsbury's 1990)
Conserving our World series (Wayland)
The Young Green Consumer's Guide by John Elkington and Julia Hales (Gollancz, 1990)
Gaia Atlas of Planetary Management (Pan, 1985)
The Green Detective series Caring for Planet Earth by Barbara Holland and Hazel Lucas (Lion, 1990)
Earthwatch by Penny Horton (BBC, 1990)
Travels in Search of Endangered Species by Jeremy Mallinson (David and Charles, 1989)
The Environment by Adam Markham (Wayland, 1988)
The Greenpeace Book of Antarctica by John May (Dorling Kindersley, 1988)
Exploiting the Sea by Malcolm Penny (Wayland, 1990)
Pollution and Conservation by Malcolm Penny (Wayland, 1988)
Jungles and Rainforests by Theodore Roland-Entwistle (Wayland, 1987)
Blueprint for a Green Planet by John Seymour and Herbert Giradet (Dorling Kindersley, 1987)
The Conservation Project Book by Hilary Thomas (Hodder & Stoughton, 1990)
Wildlife at Risk series (Wayland)

Picture Credits